MANCHESTER UNITED

A RANDOM HISTORY

• MANCHESTER UNITED •

An exclusive edition for

for all your gift books and gift stationery

This edition first published in Great Britain in 2023 by Allsorted Ltd, Watford, Herts, UK WD19 4BG

The facts and statistics in this book are correct up to the end of the 2022/23 season. The data comes from publicly available sources and is presented as correct as far as our knowledge allows. The opinions in this book are personal and individual and are not affiliated to the football club in any way. Any views or opinions represented in this book are personal and belong solely to the book author and do not represent those of people, institutions or organisations that the football club or publisher may or may not be associated with in professional or personal capacity, unless explicitly stated. Any views or opinions are not intended to malign any religious, ethnic group, club, organisation, company or individual.

© Susanna Geoghegan Gift Publishing
Author: Magnus Allan
Cover design: Milestone Creative
Contents design: Bag of Badgers Ltd
Illustrations: Ludovic Sallé

ISBN: 978-1-915902-07-8

Printed in China

★ CONTENTS ★

"IN ALL MODESTY, MY
SUMMING UP OF 1955/6
AND 1956/7 MUST BE
THAT NO CLUB IN THE
COUNTRY COULD LIVE
WITH MANCHESTER
UNITED."

Matt Busby puts it in a nutshell.

★ INTRODUCTION: ★

FOUR GREAT PERIODS … SO FAR

Manchester United has had four periods of success over its 145-year history. In the early 20th century, the team took five years to arise from near oblivion to the First Division title for the first time, following it up with an FA Cup and then a second title. Four decades later, the Busby Babes were hitting their stride with three titles and an FA Cup before eight of them were lost in the Munich air crash. Busby didn't give up and rebuilt the team, leading them to two more league titles and becoming the first English team to conquer European football. Most recently, Manchester United became the pre-eminent team of the 1990s and 2000s, when scarcely a year went by without honours of some kind.

The level of success during the first two decades of the Premier League era would be virtually impossible to sustain, but of all the clubs in all the world, Manchester United have the foundations in place that will help them reclaim their spot at the top.

They don't have an absolute right to be there, though, and

what United's many teams have shown down the years is knowing that what makes the difference between 'good' and 'great' is hard work. But they've also shown, time and time again, that they understand football is a form of entertainment: you can grind out a win – and sometimes you have to – but if you want to be great, if you want to enjoy the crowd's true adulation when you have the chance, you need to win with a little bit of panache.

It's sometimes tempting to think that United have had four great team eras – the one at the start of the 20th century, the ones in the 1950s and 1960s, and the one that delighted fans throughout the 1990s and 2000s – but the reality is that the team changes with each passing year; it evolves with each player who moves on and each player who joins.

What remains constant, though, is the philosophy of the club; in the case of Manchester United, that philosophy was developed during its very earliest days, when football had only recently embraced passing. It's a philosophy that works from box to box, that lets players play, and most of all, it provides what the fans want to see: attack, attack, attack-attack-attack ...

IN 1980, IPSWICH TOWN BEAT MANCHESTER UNITED 6-0, DESPITE THE UNITED KEEPER STOPPING THREE PENALTIES ALONG THE WAY (ONE WAS A RETAKE). UNITED GOT THEIR REVENGE IN 1995, WALLOPING IPSWICH 9-0, ONE OF ONLY FOUR 9-0 VICTORIES IN THE HISTORY OF THE PREMIER LEAGUE. NO TEAM HAS YET ACHIEVED A 10-0 VICTORY IN THE PREMIER LEAGUE.

•MANCHESTER UNITED•

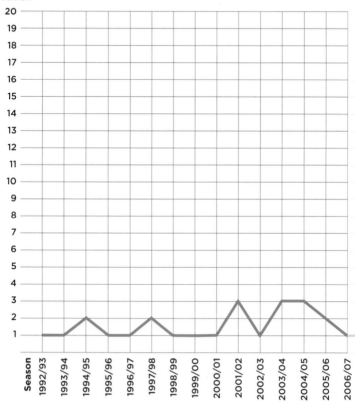

Position

Season

8

PREMIER LEAGUE
★ FINAL POSITIONS ★

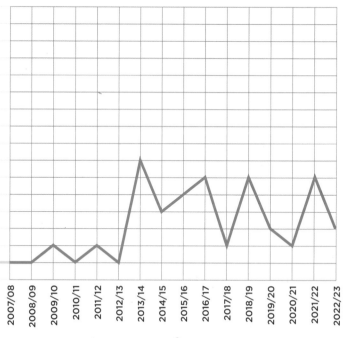

★ GEORGE WALL ★

There are those who say that the great Manchester United side of the mid- to late-1900s was built on the backbone of a team that Manchester City created, but, objectively, most people can see there was far more to it than that. Among the many cases for the defence: George Wall.

Wall played in various youth teams in his native north-east at the turn of the century before joining Second Division's Barnsley in 1903, where his form as an attacker caught the eye of Ernest Mangnall's scouts. He moved from South Yorkshire to United in 1906 and stayed until 1915.

He scored on debut, helped United gain promotion from the Second Division and played a key role in the titles and trophies that followed. He is one of the players that set the template for United, making flowing runs down the left wing that led to 100 goals in 319 appearances in all competitions.

He joined Oldham when he returned from World War I, and he kept playing until the late 1920s.

NEWTON'S LAWS: ★ THE COMBINATION ★

The earliest rules of association football were defined and codified in south-east London in 1863 by a group of schools and amateur football clubs that were sick of having long conversations to agree the rules before every match. It was slow to catch on in the south of England but spread like wildfire in the north, where the working classes wanted a break from their dark satanic mills and a bit of a run about in the fresh air. Not that the air was always very fresh at North Road or Bank Street (see page 30)

Teams were often set up around factories and, in 1878, the esteemed Carriage and Wagon department of the Newton Heath depot of the Lancashire and Yorkshire Railway (LYR) got in on the act. They spent a lot of time looking for a name, but eventually settled on Newton Heath LYR Football Club. Which did what it said on the tin, really.

They spent their formative years playing other

departments, including those crazy kids from the Motive Power Division, who were known, quite superbly, as Newton Heath Loco. They also played teams from other railways.

After a decade, Newton Heath LYR, sometimes known as 'the Heathians' or 'the Heathens', felt that they had honed their skills enough to play at a higher level, and the team became a founding member of The Combination. Despite sounding like something from a wrestling federation, The Combination was set up by a group of teams from across the Midlands and the north that hadn't managed to join the Football League.

Unfortunately, despite a lot of attention from an increasingly football-hungry audience, The Combination was plagued by poor management and communication. It was wound up without finishing its first season.

★ ERNEST MANGNALL ★

Born in Bolton in 1866, Ernest Mangnall kept goal as an amateur for Bolton Wanderers, and then he enjoyed a moderately successful period as manager of Burnley. If by 'moderately successful' you mean getting them relegated to Second Division in his first season, and then steering them to third, ninth and then bottom over the next three years.

To be fair, the relegation to the Second Division wasn't really on him because he'd only taken the job with a month left of the season, but he was lucky that there wasn't a Third Division at the time. Burnley were forced to go through the ignominy of applying for re-election to the Second Division (which is how things were done back in the day), but Mangnall decided to move on to bigger and better things.

He joined Manchester United as its secretary (these were the days before managers were a thing) and led them out of the Second Division – and then made them champions two years later in 1908. And again in 1911.

He then went and did something that has never been done before or since: he left United to join one of the other clubs in Manchester. This weirdly means that he was leading Manchester United when they moved into Old Trafford and Manchester City when they moved into Maine Road. Around 40,000 people came to his final game in charge, a Manchester derby at Old Trafford on 7 September 1912. City won it by a single goal.

He is the only manager to have led both the red and the blue sides of the city, although Mourinho is probably desperate to try to follow in his footsteps.

WHEN THE BUSBY BABES WON THE LEAGUE TITLE FOR MANCHESTER UNITED IN 1956, THE AVERAGE AGE OF THE TEAM WAS 21.

"IF YOU WANT ME TO RULE OUT EVER BEING MANCHESTER UNITED MANAGER, I CAN'T. SPECIAL CLUBS NEED SPECIAL MANAGERS, SO IN THEORY IT COULD WORK."

José Mourinho leaves people wondering if he's special offer or bargain basement. The Portuguese for hubris is arrogância, apparently.

NEWTON'S LAWS: A DALLIANCE WITH ★ THE ALLIANCE ★

Information is a little scant, but from the sound of things, there was a meeting held shortly after the winding up of The Combination in 1889 ('shortly after' being basically two minutes later – in the room next door) to set up the Football Alliance. Newton Heath LYR became one of nine founding members, alongside Small Heath (who later became Birmingham City FC), The Wednesday (who later became Sheffield Wednesday) and Grimsby Town (who still play as Grimsby Town).

They say that these days football has become a big money sport and that there are astonishing rewards on offer for the winners of the big competitions. It could be that it was the Football Alliance that started that tradition: to the victor the spoils – and in the case of the Football Alliance, the victor would win a blue silk flag, with a white border, 3.7 metres by 1.8 metres, emblazoned with the words 'Alliance Champions' on it. It doesn't sound like much, but the three winners of the Football Alliance – The Wednesday, Stoke and Nottingham Forest – still have their victories listed in the 'Honours' sections of their Wikipedia pages.

Newton Heath LYR came eighth, ninth and second during the three years that they participated, with the final result enabling them to be elected to the Football League. This was the year that the Football Alliance metamorphosed into the Football League's Second Division, so Newton Heath LYR can claim to have been part of the First Division's inaugural season, even if they didn't technically play in the first three years of the Football League. Ever get the feeling that history goes out of its way to be complicated?

★ JOHNNY CAREY ★

In the days before the internet, news tended to swirl around by word of mouth before being picked up and made official by newspapers. The most important headlines would be written on sandwich boards and put up outside newsagents. When 17-year-old Johnny Carey first arrived in Manchester he was excited to see that the newspapers already had the scoop, with sandwich boards proclaiming, 'United sign star'. He rushed into the shop to buy a paper and was somewhat crushed to discover that he wasn't actually the star in question.

There are two things that should have consoled him.

Firstly, he did get a mention in the final two lines of the article, so he got to see his name in print – which is always a thrill.

Secondly, and more importantly, the star that the article focused on was Ernie Thompson, who signed from Blackburn Rovers to great excitement but only played three games for United. Meanwhile, in a career interrupted by World War II, Carey made 304 league appearances and captained the side from 1946 to 1953. In the 1937/38 season he helped United get back into the First Division. He also helped United win the FA Cup in 1948, the First

Division in 1951/52 and the Charity Shield at the start of the 1952/53 season. So, in the big scheme of things, Thompson may have had the lion's share of an article that also announced Carey joining United, but in a brief book about Manchester United that's written three-quarters of a century later, Thompson is mentioned in passing while Carey gets a whole section to himself.

Annoyingly from the point of view of a simple narrative, before winning the league for the third time in 1951/52, Carey led United to second in four of the preceding five years. The one year they didn't come second, 1949/50, they came fourth, only three points off the pace and with a better goal average than Wolverhampton Wanderers and Sunderland who came second and third, respectively. To be fair, at the time it was only two points for a win so United would have had to win two more games to have come neatly second. (Three points for a win didn't come into English football until 1981 when influential *Match of the Day* presenter – is there any other sort – Jimmy Hill proposed it as a way of encouraging teams to go for a win rather than settle for a draw.) So, anyway, in the ideal world of the story, United would have come second for five consecutive years, but frankly the real world is just never as neat as you might hope.

Carey also played regularly for Ireland in his international career. There were two Ireland teams at this time; one covering Northern Ireland, and one covering the whole of the island. Carey played for both teams. He also went on to manage several teams, including Blackburn Rovers (twice), Everton and Nottingham Forest.

MANCHESTER UNITED HAVE ENJOYED RUNNER-UP POSITION THE JOINT HIGHEST NUMBER OF TIMES, IN 1956/57, 1957/58, 1975/76, 1978/79, 1994/95, 2004/05, 2006/07 AND 2017/18. THEY SHARE THE ACCOLADE WITH CHELSEA AND EVERTON.

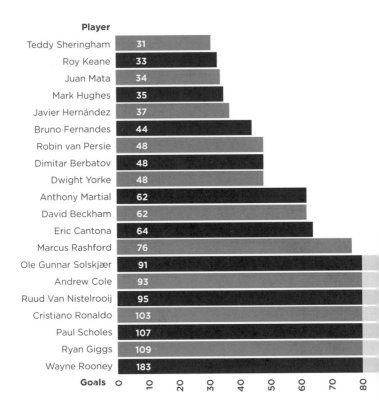

Player

Player	Goals
Teddy Sheringham	31
Roy Keane	33
Juan Mata	34
Mark Hughes	35
Javier Hernández	37
Bruno Fernandes	44
Robin van Persie	48
Dimitar Berbatov	48
Dwight Yorke	48
Anthony Martial	62
David Beckham	62
Eric Cantona	64
Marcus Rashford	76
Ole Gunnar Solskjær	91
Andrew Cole	93
Ruud Van Nistelrooij	95
Cristiano Ronaldo	103
Paul Scholes	107
Ryan Giggs	109
Wayne Rooney	183

Goals 0 10 20 30 40 50 60 70 80

MAN UTD'S LEADING PREMIER LEAGUE
★ GOAL SCORERS ★

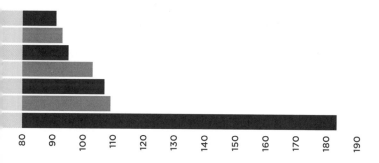

★ MATT BUSBY ★

Matt Busby played for Manchester City and then Liverpool, but we don't need to hold that against him. United had asked City whether he was available for a transfer in 1930, but couldn't afford the fee at the time, and so he had to wait until 1945 to make it to Old Trafford as anything other than a visitor.

World War II complicated a lot of careers, but for Busby, who was approaching the end of his playing days when hostilities broke out, it gave him the chance to serve as a football coach in the Army Physical Training Corps. This let him develop his theories and when the war ended, after briefly returning to Liverpool, he came up the ship canal to Old Trafford.

He brought with him a new way of working, making sure that he was involved not only in picking the team but also having a say in signings and direct involvement in training. He said it would take him five years to turn the club around – and that was how long he was given. United had spent most of the 1930s busily hopping between First and Second Divisions, and given the dire state the club was in after Old Trafford was extensively damaged during the 1940s, the club's leadership was not really in a position to argue with Busby's demands.

He took the team to second in the 1946/47 season, and again in 1947/48, and again in 1948/49, slipped to fourth in 1949/50, got back up to second in 1950/51 and then, at last, captured the elusive title in 1951/52 – six years into his reign and 41 years since United had last won the league. He went on to lead United to further league wins in 1955/56 and 1956/57.

After the Munich air tragedy in 1958 that claimed the lives of eight Manchester United players and 14 other people, he rebuilt the team and led them back to the top of the league twice more, as well as winning the European Cup in 1967/68.

He stayed in post until the end of the 1969/70 season (returning briefly in the 1970/71 season) and retired as one of the greatest leaders in the history of English, if not world, football. He retained his close links to Manchester United for the rest of his life.

"I NEVER WANTED
MANCHESTER UNITED
TO BE SECOND TO
ANYBODY. ONLY THE
BEST WOULD BE GOOD
ENOUGH."

Mission accomplished,
Matt Busby.

THE STADIUMS: NORTH ROAD AND ★ BANK STREET ★

Newton Heath LYR originally played at North Road in Newton Heath, a ground that could accommodate 12,000 to 15,000 spectators. It was right next door to the railway and apparently the team's early matches were often shrouded in smog from passing steam trains. Presumably, it did wonders for players' lung capacity.

As the team began to forge its independence from the late 1880s onwards, they gradually moved apart from the railway company, who in turn stopped subsidising it. At the same time, the pitch at North Road was owned by the religious authorities that managed Manchester cathedral and they were increasingly uncomfortable with the football club's efforts to be commercially viable by charging for tickets. So they did the normal thing when faced with an ecumenical dilemma around money: they piously whacked up the rent.

So, by the early 1890s, faced with falling subsidies, rising rents and, in 1893, an eviction notice, the club was forced to move three miles away to Bank Street in Clayton. They arrived in June 1893, but a couple of issues with the Bank Street facilities quickly became apparent. The first was that rather than being enveloped in smog from passing trains as they often were at North Road, at Bank Street they were regularly choked out by the billowing chemical smoke from nearby factories. The Clean Air Act was still more than half a century away.

As importantly, the running track around the edge of the pitch needed to be kept, which meant that the stands were further from the action. More importantly, though, the whole set-up needed to be converted from an athletics track and football pitch into an athletics track and football stadium. Which is a process that costs a large amount of money.

Developing Bank Street – which was said to be a quagmire at one end and a flint heap at the other – at the same time as professional players' wage expectations were beginning to creep up and as the club languished in the Second Division – started to put Newton Heath's finances under pressure. By 1902, they found themselves heavily in debt, in danger of eviction and under threat of being closed down by their creditors (see page 44).

BRITISH ACTOR IAN MCSHANE IS KNOWN FOR ROLES IN DEADWOOD, JOHN WICK, GAME OF THRONES AND, OF COURSE, LOVEJOY. HIS FATHER, HARRY MCSHANE, PLAYED FOR UNITED BETWEEN 1950 AND 1954, MAKING 56 LEAGUE APPEARANCES. HE LATER WORKED AS AN ANNOUNCER AT OLD TRAFFORD AND, AS A SCOUT, HE WAS RESPONSIBLE FOR BRINGING WES BROWN TO THE CLUB.

"SOME PEOPLE COME TO OLD TRAFFORD AND CAN'T SPELL FOOTBALL, LET ALONE UNDERSTAND IT. THEY HAVE A FEW DRINKS AND A PRAWN SANDWICH BUT DON'T REALISE WHAT'S HAPPENING ON THE PITCH."

Roy Keane embraces all the different kinds of football fans out there.

★ DUNCAN EDWARDS ★

Duncan Edwards was widely talked about as a generational talent, someone who has the potential to earn a name for themselves and their club, and bring a level of entertainment to others that will echo down the years.

Born in Dudley in 1936, he was spotted as a teenager and signed for Manchester United in 1952. He made 177 appearances for the club, making his debut in April 1953 as the Busby Babes began to emerge as a force to be reckoned with within English football. He played for six seasons at United, helping the team win the league in 1955/56 and 1956/57 as well as the Charity Shield in 1956 and 1957.

He also earned 18 caps for England, scoring five goals, having come through the ranks of the England Schoolboys, Under 23s and England Bs.

He lost his life at the age of 21 from the injuries he sustained during the Munich air crash in 1958, alongside 22 other passengers and crew. His pivotal role in the Busby Babes, and his talent and contributions to Manchester United as a whole, will always be celebrated by United fans.

NEWTON'S LAWS: ★ WHAT GOES UP ... ★

By 1892, Newton Heath had grown beyond its formal association with the Lancashire and Yorkshire Railway and so dropped the LYR from their name. They found themselves in the First Division of the Football League for the 1892/93 season, but despite thumping Wolverhampton Wanderers 10–1 in October, they ended the season at the bottom of the table, nine points adrift of safety.

All was not lost, though. The early rules of football can occasionally flirt with being a bit complicated, but let's try to keep it as simple as possible. The way that the Football League worked back in the day was that at the end of the season the bottom three clubs from the First Division would play the top three clubs from the Second Division in a test match. We'd probably call it a play-off today. The winners would take a place in the top flight and the losers would find themselves in the other place.

So, despite coming last and being nine points adrift, Newton Heath dismantled the Second Division champions Small Heath 5–2, beating the odds to retain their place in the First Division.

The Heathens couldn't do it twice, though, and having come last again in the 1893/94 season, this time 10 points adrift, they faced a newly formed Liverpool – who beat them 2–0. They came third in the 1894/95 season in the Second Division, but lost their test match, sixth the next season, and second the season after – but again lost their test matches (which had become two-legged affairs by this point because the stakes were high and you could sell a lot of tickets).

After that, as the 19th century gave way to the 20th, they seem to have accepted their fate as a Second Division team. Players started to take their talents elsewhere, fair-weather fans started to drift to other teams and Newton Heath started to find themselves in financial difficulties ...

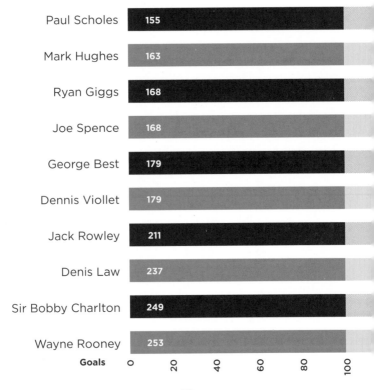

	Goals
Paul Scholes	155
Mark Hughes	163
Ryan Giggs	168
Joe Spence	168
George Best	179
Dennis Viollet	179
Jack Rowley	211
Denis Law	237
Sir Bobby Charlton	249
Wayne Rooney	253

MAN UTD'S LEADING ALL-TIME GOAL SCORERS

★ ★

(ALL COMPETITIONS)

★ SIR BOBBY CHARLTON ★

Sir Bobby Charlton is a player who embodies Manchester United's footballing philosophy, running the game from the midfield – graceful, assertive and attack-minded. He's part of a footballing dynasty, with his uncle Jackie Milburn (a stalwart of Newcastle United between 1943 and 1957) and brother Jack Charlton (playing for Leeds between 1952 and 1973).

Bobby Charlton joined United in 1956 and stayed until 1973 (retiring on the same day as his brother). He racked up 606 league appearances and 199 league goals.

Born and raised in Northumberland, his mum wanted him to keep up his apprenticeship as an electrical engineer, so he was invited to join United as an amateur. It was his talent as a footballer that shone, though, and he went professional in the autumn of 1954, rising through the ranks and making his first-team debut against namesake Londoners Charlton Athletic two years later. He marked the event with a brace.

Charlton survived the Munich air crash in February 1958 that claimed the lives of 23 people, including eight of his teammates, as they returned from a victorious European Cup match in Yugoslavia.

He then played a key role in Manchester United's rebuilding process, helping them win the FA Cup in 1963, then the League itself in both 1965 and 1967, before capping it all with a victory in the European Cup in 1968, where he scored twice.

Charlton made 106 appearances for England, scoring 49 goals. This included playing a pivotal role in the semi-finals and final of the 1966 World Cup. Which England won. He has maintained his long association with United and enjoys an afternoon on the terraces at Old Trafford to this day.

OLE GUNNAR SOLSKJÆR SCORED FOUR GOALS IN 12 MINUTES DURING AN 8-1 DEMOLITION OF NOTTINGHAM FOREST IN 1999.

"I CAN'T HELP WONDERING WHAT I'M GOING TO DO WHEN ALL THIS ENDS."

Sir Bobby wondered about life after football in 1970. No matter what he's done with the rest of his time, he's been at Old Trafford for as many matches as possible in the half century since his retirement. So at least his Saturday afternoons have always been sorted.

NEWTON'S LAWS: DOGGED BY FINANCIAL ★ DIFFICULTIES ★

It's a fascinating thing, but when you look back into the history books of many clubs, there's often a random story involving a dog. Here's Manchester United's.

By the early 1900s, Newton Heath were struggling financially, so they held a four-day grand bazaar in the St James' Hall on Oxford Road to raise funds. One of the attractions was Major, a St Bernard dog that belonged to Newton's captain, Harry Stafford. The dog was often seen mooching around the Bank Street terraces on match days with a collection tin around his neck.

There are long versions and short versions of this particular shaggy dog story, but the short version goes that one evening after the bazaar, the dog ambled off, collection tin attached, and, in the nature of St Bernards everywhere, followed his snout to the very finest restaurant in the area. Once there, he started politely asking the patrons for any food that they might have to spare. They are not an intimidating dog, your St Bernard, but they are fairly sizeable and they are pretty good at making what they want very clear, applying a deceptively simple strategy that involves a fiendishly efficient combination of staring and drooling very heavily.

Having his supper at the restaurant was one John Henry Davies, self-made estate agent, brewer, innkeeper and Victorian gentleman of business. The sort of fellow who owned a bowler hat and wasn't afraid to wear it. History doesn't record what he was intending to eat, but let's take a guess at sausages – and a second guess that Major did all right out of the whole thing. Quite right.

Davies decided that he wanted to buy the dog for his daughter's birthday, so he tracked down Stafford to negotiate. Stafford initially refused to sell his dog, but the pair got to talking and, in the end, Davies decided to help the football club, clearing its debts, becoming chairman and taking ownership of Major in the process.

One of his first moves was to rename the club, and at the end of the 1901/02 season Manchester United was born.

Davies completely restructured the club, and by 1906 the club could invest in a covered stand for the Bank Street stadium, the first in the country. This kept the rain off and brought match-day capacity up to 50,000.

This did not satisfy Davies' ambitions, though. He wanted a stadium that could welcome 100,000 people on match day, and with Manchester's population on the rise and labour laws changing to give workers a little more free time, he felt it was time to move somewhere bigger. Old Trafford beckoned ...

FERGIE TIME IS APPARENTLY REAL, WITH 81 GOALS BEING SCORED IN TIME ADDED ON AT THE END OF A MATCH DURING HIS REIGN.

"WE LEARNED A LOT FROM UNITED TODAY, INCLUDING HOW TO COUNT."

Shrewsbury manager Kevin Ratcliffe reflects on a pre-season friendly against Manchester United in July 2000 that came with a less than friendly 8-1 result.

★ DAVID HERD ★

David 'Hot Shot' Herd joined Manchester United from Arsenal at the start of the 1961/62 season, playing a key role in the team's success during the decade. All told, he made 265 appearances for the club, delivering 145 goals. He scored his debut goal for United against Chelsea.

He was raised in Manchester, where his father Alec Herd spent 15 years playing for Manchester City from 1933. He was, however, born in Lanarkshire after Herd senior sent his wife back over the border to give birth. As a result, young David would be eligible to play for Scotland, which he did five times. The two Herds played together briefly at Stockport County, where David started his career and Alec played his last few games.

Once Herd Junior reached United, he formed a solid striking partnership with Denis Law, delivering an average of 21 goals per season during the seven that he spent at Old Trafford. That average rises to 24 if you discount his final season, when he spent most of the time on the sidelines with a broken leg.

In any other team, in any other era, Herd might be the name that everyone remembers, but he was part of a formidable United attack that included George Best,

Bobby Charlton, as well as Law. He seemed to be happy to let them take the limelight, so long as he kept getting on the scoresheet.

Herd left United for Stoke City before crossing the Irish Sea to play briefly for Waterford, where former United comrade Seamus Brennan was player-manager. He tried his hand at management himself when he retired, but spent most of his time running car garages around Manchester.

United played Stoke the day after he died in 2016, with both teams wearing black armbands in his memory.

THE 'CLASS OF '92' PLAYED MORE THAN 3,000 MATCHES FOR MANCHESTER UNITED. YOU'LL WIN NOTHING WITH KIDS ...

"I HAVE BEEN A
MANCHESTER UNITED
FAN ALL MY LIFE AND
FULFILLED EVERY
DREAM I'VE EVER HAD.
I AM DISAPPOINTED
THAT MY PLAYING
DAYS ARE AT AN END.
HOWEVER, IT COMES
TO US ALL AND IT'S
KNOWING WHEN THAT
TIME IS AND FOR ME
THAT TIME IS NOW."

Gary Neville shows the world
how to bow out gracefully.

51

THE GLORIOUS
★ FIRST TITLE ★

The newly christened Manchester United brought in Ernest Mangnall (see page 14) to serve as their secretary (a role that slowly evolved into manager), and things started to look upwards. In 1902/03 they achieved fifth in the Second Division, 13 points off the promotion places, but significantly better than the year before when they were in a relegation fight and only stayed up on goal difference. (Technically at the time it was known as a re-election fight and United only stayed up on goal average, but you get the drift. England continued to use goal average as a tie-breaker until 1975, when they adopted goal difference.)

In the 1903/04 season they improved again, coming third with only two points separating them from being promoted as champions. It was a similar story in 1904/05, but then in 1905/06 they came second after Bristol City and rose into the First Division for the first time since the 1893/94 season.

The next season was a tight one, with Manchester United coming eighth but only three points off third, six off second and nine off the top spot.

But then came the 1907/08 season ... They started with three wins, stumbled slightly and then went on a run of 10 matches without loss, which put them comfortably in the box seat for the title run in. The papers were full of breathless cliches in eloquent Victorian language. By the end of it all, they were nine points clear of second-placed Aston Villa.

There are some who like to taint this victory, claiming that the backbone of the squad was made up of players that had been sold by Manchester City. There is no denying that Mangnall did buy four players from Manchester City, and it was indeed a fine bit of business that really bolstered the United team. But ask yourself: why did City have to sell the players? It turns out that City were forced into selling their players because of financial irregularities.

Anyway, Manchester United followed victory in the league with victory in the very first Charity Shield at the start of the 1908/09 season, and then washed it all down with victory in the FA Cup. The template was set.

★ NOBBY STILES ★

Nobby Stiles, the man who danced around Wembley with the Jules Rimet Cup in one hand (some say he was holding his false teeth in the other), played for Manchester United for 11 years, and won two league titles and the European Cup.

Manchester born and bred, Stiles joined United in 1960 after Matt Busby recognised his talent and honed him into a holding midfielder. He holds the rare honour of having been able to man-mark Portuguese legend Eusébio into obsolescence in both the 1966 World Cup semi-final and Manchester United's European Cup victory two years later. And he did it with efficiency, rather than maliciously, by simply preventing the man getting the ball and running with it.

He went into coaching and management as his career came to a close, and continued his association with Manchester United, helping the 'Class of '92' as they worked their way towards the Youth FA Cup.

In the days of footballers being paid tens of thousands of pounds a day, it's hard to comprehend that Stiles had to sell much of his football memorabilia in later life, including his World Cup winner's medal, to support himself financially. It's a reminder of how short a footballer's career can be.

THE STADIUMS:
★ OLD TRAFFORD ★

Old Trafford, Bobby Charlton's theatre of dreams, the very epicentre of English football ... there are newer, shinier stadiums, but none of them have the heritage of the home of Manchester United.

United moved into the stadium late in 1909, fresh from their first victories in the FA Cup and the First Division. The site had a lot of things going for it. Firstly, there were the rail lines that had been built to support the nearby Old Trafford cricket ground, which meant fans would be able to make their way to the ground relatively easily. Secondly, the land was already owned by another of John Henry Davies' businesses, so the land could change hands relatively cheaply. Thirdly, there was a lot of industrial activity around Trafford Park – and many of the businesses gave their workers a half day on Saturday. Good transport, cheap land and an audience waiting to be entertained.

United timed their move from Bank Street exceptionally well. The main stand was blown down in a gale just after the team moved to Old Trafford, although the reserve team continued to use the site until the lease expired at the start of 1912.

Like most football clubs in the early- to mid-20th century, United turned to Archibald Leitch to design and build the stadium. The original plan was that Old Trafford would be able to host 100,000 spectators, although this was reduced to 80,000 when costs started to spiral.

Liverpool were the first team to be welcomed to the new stadium, but despite the home team having a one goal lead at half-time, they proved that they weren't very gracious guests and had the audacity to beat United 4–3. That was just a teething issue, though; United finished their first season at Old Trafford with only one home defeat. In the following season, they won the league title for the second time.

Manchester United's home was both well conceived and well built; as a result, it did not need major work between its completion and the 1940s, following extensive damage during World War II.

Rebuilding was a slower process than the original construction and put quite a strain on United's finances. No matches were played at Old Trafford between 1939 and 1949, with Manchester City very graciously allowing Manchester United to play their home matches at Maine Road. (City did okay out of the arrangement according to the accountants, but, to be fair, you wouldn't expect it any other way.)

Capacity declined during the post-war period as safety made its way up the agenda, both for the club and footballing authorities, with fans still lamenting the loss of the old Stretford End in the mid-1990s. However, extensions to Old Trafford mean that its current 74,000 capacity isn't too far below pre-war levels.

Various plans to overhaul the stadium have been discussed in recent years, but finding somewhere suitable for United to play while the stadium is rebuilt – or a suitable site for the team to move to – have held back changes so far. In the meantime, Old Trafford remains a place where most players and fans would love to be but fear to come.

"PAUL SCHOLES IS MY
FAVOURITE PLAYER.
HE EPITOMISES
THE SPIRIT OF
MANCHESTER UNITED
AND EVERYTHING
THAT IS GOOD ABOUT
FOOTBALL,"

says Sir Bobby Charlton, a man
who knows.

★ DENIS LAW ★

Denis Law is the only Scottish football player ever to have won the *Ballon d'or*, which he did in 1964. He'd started playing professionally at Huddersfield Town in 1956, where he worked with future Liverpool manager Bill Shankly. When Shankly left for Merseyside, he wanted to take Law with him, but, by all accounts, Liverpool couldn't afford Town's demands. There was also interest from Matt Busby's Manchester United, but it was Manchester City that secured his signature, and Law moved over the Pennines in 1961 for an English record of £55,000 (which Huddersfield spent on some of those new-fangled floodlights).

After a year at Manchester City, he went to Torino to try his hand at the Italian leagues, but is said to have had a torrid time so after a couple of twists and turns he ended up doing the right thing and joining United ... where he flew, scoring after a mere seven minutes on his debut. In the next season he scored goals in all competitions, and in the season after that won the *Ballon d'or*.

Law left United after 11 years, having scored 237 goals in 404 games in all competitions. He also won two league titles and the FA Cup.

★ MAN UTD'S LEADING

Season	Player	Goals
2002/03	Ruud van Nistelrooij	25
2003/04	Ruud van Nistelrooij	20
2004/05	Wayne Rooney	11
2005/06	Ruud van Nistelrooij	21
2006/07	Cristiano Ronaldo	17
2007/08	Cristiano Ronaldo	31
2008/09	Cristiano Ronaldo	18
2009/10	Wayne Rooney	26
2010/11	Dimitar Berbatov	20
2011/12	Wayne Rooney	27
2012/13	Robin van Persie	26
2013/14	Wayne Rooney	17
2014/15	Wayne Rooney	12
2015/16	Anthony Martial	11
2016/17	Zlatan Ibrahimovic	17
2017/18	Romelu Lukaku	16
2018/19	Paul Pogba	13
2019/20	Anthony Martial/Marcus Rashford	17
2020/21	Bruno Fernandes	18
2021/22	Cristiano Ronaldo	18
2022/23	Marcus Rashford	17

Goals   0   5   10

GOAL SCORERS BY SEASON ★

(PREMIER LEAGUE)

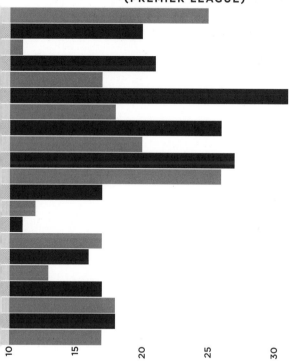

WHY WAS THE FOOTBALL LEAGUE ★ FORMED? ★

These days we take the Football League system for granted. It's just there, every August, shiny and new and full of hope; every February, it is creaky and jaded and down to a couple of teams that might just be able to stay the distance while everybody else slugs it out for European football positions and pretends they are happy about it.

But why did the Football League happen? Why didn't football teams just carry on playing locally? What's the point of it all?

The short answer, you'll be astonished to hear, is money.

In the 1870s, football was an amateur sport and it was illegal to pay footballers. When football swept to the northern cities, various clubs started to find ways around this amateur status; for example, by offering good jobs to people who were half decent at chasing a ball round a field. Mayors and other dignitaries started competing to get the best players into their teams, and so players started to be offered better jobs if they'd just move over the Pennines, down the Manchester Ship Canal or up to somewhere near the Tyne.

This was all illegal, so it had to be done under the table and, as a result, it was open to abuse. It was also fairly obvious what was happening.

As a result, the authorities gradually accepted that they had to start loosening the rules, and in 1885 it became legal to be a professional footballer in England.

The trouble was that it now meant football clubs had to find a way of paying a full squad of footballers, which is why a string of football teams including Newton Heath found themselves struggling financially at the turn of the twentieth century.

The best way to keep the creditors at bay was to sell lots of tickets on match days, and the best way to do that was to make sure the football on offer was entertaining. This was a big change; in the amateur era, people were playing for their own enjoyment, but once you turn professional and are selling tickets, you need to provide enjoyment for the people coming through the turnstiles rather than just the people on the pitch.

Meanwhile, north of the border, it was still illegal to be paid for playing football, so a generation of Scottish players came south to seek glory and modest fortunes by joining English teams. Players such as Newton Heath's Bob Donaldson, Fred Erentz and Willie Stewart brought with them a different approach to the game – passing the ball as well as dribbling it, which changed the way that the game was played – added new strategies and made it much more interesting to watch. By making it more interesting to watch, the teams sold more tickets.

The Football League was formed as a way of making sure that the bigger football clubs of the day had a decent quality of opposition, that a victory gave the fans something to cheer about and a reason to keep spending their wages on coming to matches.

In some ways, though, it also meant that teams in the Football League had to make sure they could afford to move their squads around the country to pay for away games – because 130 years ago there weren't any motorways, and getting around the country was slow and expensive. Train tickets, hotel rooms, meals while the players were on the road ... clubs needed to sell even more tickets to pay for it all.

The best way to do this was to make sure you could attract the best players, and while late-19th-century footballers were, of course, mostly motivated by quality-of-life considerations, money was also a factor. In short, teams needed to offer better wages than the opposition down the road to attract the best talent. To do that, they needed to make sure they had cash coming in. So they needed to sell even more tickets.

Basically, the Football League created a self-perpetuating loop that ultimately led to the creation of the gigantic international brands that we have today. It's not perfect, but you've got to admit that it kind of works.

MANCHESTER UNITED'S WORST EVER LEAGUE POSITION WAS 20TH PLACE IN THE SECOND DIVISION IN 1933/34.

★ GEORGE BEST ★

George Best is one of those players who makes you smile when you think of them on the pitch. He was spotted playing in Belfast as a boy by a Manchester United scout who sent a telegram to Matt Busby that ready simply, "I think I've found you a genius."

He joined United at 17 and stayed at Old Trafford from 1963 to 1974, finding the net 179 times in 470 appearances in all competitions.

Football was a very physical game at the time, and sometimes defenders would use that physicality to stop the very best players from playing. Busby saw that this could be a problem for young Best and had him trained to be able to outmanoeuvre defenders. They couldn't land a kick if he'd already moved on.

For a sense of quite how Best's movement off the ball could confound an opposition defence, it's worth looking up a 1965 Top of the Pops performance of *The Last Time* by the Rolling Stones. This was before he became known as the fifth Beatle.

Best's struggles off the pitch are well documented, but in his pomp he was United's top scorer for six consecutive seasons and one of the best football players the world has ever been lucky enough to see.

THE OPPOSITION: ★ LIVERPOOL ★

Once upon a time, there were two mighty cities. One was a port that brought in raw materials from around the world; the other was a centre of industry, taking those raw materials and turning them into all manner of items that were then sent back to the port and shipped out around the world.

One day, the industrial city decided to improve its efficiency by digging a canal that was wide enough for ships so that the raw materials it needed could come straight to its factories and mills. This worked out very nicely for the industrial city, but the port city was slightly aggrieved about the whole thing because some of its people lost their jobs as a result.

At around the same time, these two cities, let's call them Liverpool and Manchester for the sake of argument, were setting up football teams, and so the economic rivalry spilled over a bit on to the terraces. Over the years, though, one football team in each city became particularly well regarded, and there have been many mighty clashes between the two teams in red down the years.

They have played each other around 240 times. While it's fairly evenly balanced, Manchester United have shaved it by winning just under 40% of the time; Liverpool have won a shade over a third of the time. Draws make up the balance.

Looking at the Premier League, the stats reflect United's dominance over the first three decades of the competition. United have won just under half of the two teams' encounters, while just under 25% have ended in a draw. You can do the rest of the maths for yourself. Nearly a third of matches between the two deliver four or more goals, and there have only been five turgid 0–0s.

It could be said that more recently results have been a little more in favour of the Merseyside team, but no one's really got the time or the inclination to investigate.

There are those who suggest that the rivalry between the two cities dates back even further, back to the start of the Industrial Revolution, but there is another possibility. It could be that the elites of London have always encouraged the rivalry between the two cities because they are easier to control if they are divided ... It could be that the elites of Eton deliberately gave up their 19th-century control over football and sent it to the north-west to keep the working classes from rising together. Perhaps ... but given the state of what Eton's been putting out over the last few years, there's very little evidence that they are all that clever.

"LIVERPOOL - 30 MILES FROM GREATNESS."

Visiting United supporters
arrive at Anfield in 2003 with
a banner that kindly reminds
Liverpool fans how close they
are to Old Trafford.

★ ALEX STEPNEY ★

Alex Stepney started playing professionally at Millwall in 1963, where he spent three years prior joining Chelsea. He spent three months at Chelsea before turning his back on the capital and coming to the spiritual home of football in the north-west.

He was signed by Sir Matt Busby when Manchester United found themselves in a goalkeeping predicament after Harry Gregg was injured. Stepney's clean sheet on debut against Manchester City was a good way to open his account and win the support of the Stretford End.

He helped United clinch the title in 1966/67 and then played a vital role in the team's victorious European Cup run in the 1967/68 season. In the final against Benfica at Wembley, he made it look easy to stop a Eusébio shot from inside the box in the dying seconds of normal time (it was the one moment when the Portuguese legend slipped Nobby Stiles' marking). Eusébio took a moment to stop and applaud Stepney's skill.

It wasn't all European glory, though. The club was relegated (five points adrift from safety) at the end of the

1973/74 season, although they bounced back as Second Division champions the next season, with Stepney adding wisdom and experience to a very young United squad. Once back in the top flight, he helped the team come in as runners-up in the FA Cup in 1975/76 and then lift the trophy a year later for the fourth time, denying Liverpool the treble in the process.

He left United after 12 years at the end of the 1977/78 season to play for a couple of years in the US. In total, he played 546 games for United and was the last remaining player to have worked with Sir Matt Busby at Old Trafford.

MANCHESTER UNITED WERE THE FIRST ENGLISH CLUB TO WIN THE DOMESTIC TREBLE IN 1998/99.

"MANCHESTER UNITED ARE LOOKING TO FRANK STAPLETON TO PULL SOME MAGIC OUT OF THE FIRE."

Jimmy Hill was a man of many talents; one of which, unfortunately, was the ability to mercilessly mangle the English language. Iron out of fire, magic out of hat.

HOW THE STRIP
★ HAS CHANGED ★

Newton Heath LYR and Newton Heath had worn a variety of kit colours down the years, switching between white with a blue cord, green and gold, and red and white. There's no recorded reason for these colour changes in the history books, although white shirts were presumably cheapest, which would have been a major consideration when setting up a works team, and green and gold were the corporate colours of the Lancashire and Yorkshire Railway (who by all accounts had a fiercely protective 19th-century branding division that you crossed at your peril) (maybe).

Again, history is a little fuzzy but in 1902, the newly rechristened Manchester United adopted red shirts, white shorts and black socks, potentially to make a clean break with the team's past. The Heathians had played in white shirts with navy blue shorts for their last six seasons, and very few teams in the Football League were playing in red shirts at the time, so it might be as simple as that.

While the team has predominantly stuck to the colour scheme ever since, there was a brief period in 1922 when they started playing in white shirts with a red 'V' across the chest. This was the decision of new manager John Chapman (officially the sixth person to hold the position), and was the same colour scheme used by the Airdrieonians Football Club where Chapman had previously worked. To be fair, it was also the alternative strip that United had used for the victorious 1909 FA Cup campaign when they were playing Bristol City, who also played in red – so perhaps he simply found the 1909 kit lying about in a cupboard and decided to give it a go.

Chapman steered United back into the First Division in 1924/25 but was then removed from his post in 1926 having been suspended for improper conduct by the Football Association (FA). There is no record of what he'd done, but United went back into red as quickly as they could once he'd moved on.

There was then a very brief dalliance with a white and cherry-red hooped affair in the 1933/34 season, but this was deemed to be a ludicrous diversion and coincided with United narrowly avoiding relegation to the Third Division by a single point. They moved back into red for the 1934/35 season and, undoubtably as a direct consequence, rose to fifth in the Second Division the next year and were then promoted as champions a year later. The white and cherry-red shirts are probably still somewhere in a dusty sub-basement of old Trafford in a locked, nailed-shut drawer marked 'DO NOT OPEN'.

United have played in red shirts ever since. We can talk about the changing colours of socks and shorts if you like, but there's no particularly fascinating story attached; they simply oscillate between white and black – potentially according to what was lucky or unlucky the year before.

MANCHESTER UNITED HAVE BEEN IN THE TOP FLIGHT OF ENGLISH FOOTBALL SINCE 1975/76.

"WHAT DO YOU THINK OF MANCHESTER UNITED'S THREE RS – ROONEY, RONALDO AND VAN NISTELROOIJ?"

Pundit Rob McCaffrey needs to either tighten his script or head back to school.

★ BRYAN ROBSON ★

Bryan Robson was the captain of the team that ended Manchester United's 26-year wait for a league title, capturing the inaugural Premier League title at the end of the 1992/93 season and starting two decades of unprecedented success.

Robson had joined United in 1981, following Ron Atkinson, his manager at West Bromwich Albion, up the M6 to Manchester. He quickly became captain, helping United win all five major titles at least once, making 465 appearances (345 of them in the league) and delivering 100 goals (74 of them in the league).

He also frequently led the England team throughout the 1980s, winning 90 caps and finding the net 26 times. He became known as Captain Marvel, scoring a hat-trick in an 8–0 drubbing of Turkey in Istanbul.

He left United in 1994 and joined Middlesborough as player-manager, beginning a career in management that took him down to Bradford City, back to the Baggies, up to Sheffield and then across a bit to Thailand.

★ OWNING THE CHARTS ★

Sometimes, when you look back into the history books, you'll find something that will make you scratch your head and ask, "Why did we used to do that?" For example, football teams used to produce songs to celebrate a decent run in the FA Cup, which was something of a fashion between the 1970s and 1990s, with Chelsea, Coventry City, Tottenham, Liverpool and West Ham all inexplicably carving an hour or so out of the training schedules to go into the recording studio and do something painfully jaunty. Whistles often featured – to emphasise the cheery footballing goodness of it all.

Some of these songs have subsequently reached legendary status (mostly for all the wrong reasons), but only Manchester United have the honour of climbing to the very pinnacle of the

British pop charts, a feat they achieved with 1994's almost supernaturally forgettable *Come On You Reds*.

But it wasn't just Britain where they hit the top spot; they did it in Denmark as well. And they got to number two in Ireland and number seven in Norway. Imagine.

To be fair, the England national team had achieved similar levels of success with *Back Home* in 1970 and the sublime *World in Motion* in 1990 (which also did pretty well internationally), but no other domestic team has shone as brightly in the hit parade as Manchester United.

We should move swiftly on before anyone mentions 1999's *Lift it High*, which sounds like it owes more than a small debt to two brothers from the other side of the city (who, to be fair, owe more than a small debt to a bunch of mop tops from the other end of the M62) ...

Mark Hughes joined the Manchester United set-up when he left school at 17 and made his first team debut three years later, finding the net, which boded well for the future. He quickly cemented a place in Ron Atkinson's first team and his 25 goals that year helped United get to fourth in the league and raise the FA Cup in 1984/85.

At the end of the following season, he left Old Trafford to go on a two-year European adventure, pulling on the shirts of Barcelona and Bayern Munich, before returning to United for slightly less than he'd left for, which always makes the accountants happy.

He spent the next seven years as the backbone of Alex Ferguson's emerging team, providing a steady stream of goals as the team transformed itself. He scored both goals in the victorious final of the European Cup Winner's Cup against former team Barcelona (although, to be fair, the first goal was a header from Steve Bruce that Hughes made sure found its way into the back of the net. Very sure). He latterly also formed a very effective partnership with Eric Cantona.

He left Old Trafford for a second time at the end of the 1994/95 season, but kept playing for several years, spending time at Chelsea, Southampton, Everton and

Blackburn Rovers. He was also capped 72 times for Wales and has subsequently stepped into management.

Hughes was born near Wrexham, which may become relevant now that AFC Wrexham have climbed back into English Football League Two. You could picture Hughes as Deadpool's long-suffering manager, stomping up and down the touchline and trying to keep the Merc with the Mouth in line. He did a decent job with Cantona. Mark Hughes and Ryan Reynolds: the Marvel team-up that the world never knew it needed.

WITH TWO GOALS TO HIS CREDIT, ALEX STEPNEY IS MANCHESTER UNITED'S MOST PROLIFIC GOAL-SCORING GOALKEEPER. NO OTHER UNITED SHOT-STOPPER HAS SCORED IN A COMPETITIVE MATCH SINCE WORLD WAR II.

"THE CENTRE FORWARD WITH THE ON-PITCH DISPOSITION OF SOMETHING LET LOOSE ON THE STREETS OF PAMPLONA."

Jim White goes all multicultural when he could simply have said that Mark Hughes was going at it like a bull in a China shop.

Player	Club
Michael Owen	Liverpool, Newcastle United, Manchester United, Stoke City
Jermain Defoe	Bournemouth, Sunderland, Tottenham Hotspur, Portsmouth, West Ham, Charlton Athletic
Robbie Fowler	Liverpool, Leeds, Manchester City, Blackburn Rovers
Thierry Henry	Arsenal
Frank Lampard	West Ham, Chelsea, Manchester City
Sergio Agüero	Manchester City
Andrew Cole	Sunderland, Portsmouth, Manchester City, Fulham, Blackburn Rovers, Manchester United, Newcastle United
Wayner Rooney	Everton, Manchester United
Harry Kane	Tottenham Hotspur
Alan Shearer	Blackburn Rovers, Newcastle United

Goals

PREMIER LEAGUE'S
★ TOP SCORERS ★

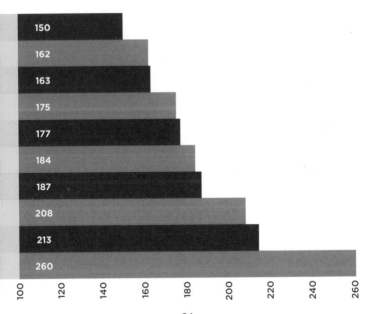

★ SIR ALEX FERGUSON ★

Alex Ferguson prowled the United touchline, masticating furiously, from 1986 to 2013. His list of achievements is world class, and his presence continues to be felt at Old Trafford a decade after his official retirement.

As a player, he enjoyed a 17-year career with a variety of Scottish clubs, including Rangers, and was the joint top goal scorer in the Scottish league in 1965/66. As his playing days came to an end, he moved into management – initially and briefly at East Stirlingshire, then at St Mirren, where he spent four years transforming them from also-rans in the Scottish Second Division to champions of the First Division (Scotland already had a Premier Division at that point).

He joined Aberdeen just before the start of the 1978/79 season, leading them to their first victory in the Scottish Premier Division a year later. In all, he delivered the Scottish Premier Division three times in 1979/80, 1983/84 and 1984/85, the Scottish Cup in 1981/82, 1982/83, 1983/84 and 1985/86, the Scottish League Cup in 1985/86, the Drybrough Cup in 1980, the European Cup Winners' Cup in 1982/83, and the European Super Cup in 1983.

In November 1986, Ferguson came south of the border

to take over at Manchester United, ushering in an age of astonishing success. It's worth taking a moment to note that he took four years to bring the first silverware to the club, and there were some on the terraces who were ready to point him towards the door.

Victory in the FA Cup in 1989/90 and then in the 1990/91 European Cup Winners' Cup started to turn doubters into believers, but it was the signing of Eric Cantona from Leeds that started to put United into contention. The team won the inaugural Premier League and, frankly, barely looked back.

There are so many factors that go into winning a trophy, but under Ferguson's leadership Manchester United went on a winning streak that lasted for more than two decades and delivered nearly 40 trophies.

"IF CHELSEA DROP POINTS, THE CAT'S OUT IN THE OPEN. AND YOU KNOW WHAT CATS ARE LIKE – SOMETIMES THEY DON'T COME HOME."

Alex Ferguson proves that not everything he said was quotable.

THE MUNICH
★ AIR CRASH ★

In February 1958, Manchester United were riding high. Matt Busby's strategy of developing youth players had paid off spectacularly and United were in the hunt for a third consecutive title in the English top flight. They were six points off the top spot, but it was only February and anything could happen in the 14 games ahead. United had not been beaten for 11 games: they had momentum on their side. They'd lifted the FA Charity Shield at the start of the season, were through to the fifth round of the FA Cup after comfortable victories against Wokington and Ipswich in the third and fourth rounds, and they'd just beaten Red Star Belgrade on aggregate to reach their second European Cup semi-final.

Back in the day, aircraft couldn't fly as far as they do today, so the flight carrying the United team back from what was then Yugoslavia had to stop off in Munich in Germany to refuel.

It was a cold winter afternoon in central Germany, and the aircraft was having a problem with one of its engines. The first two take-off attempts were aborted. The snow began to fall, and as the plane made its third attempt at taking off, it hit slush that had accumulated at the end of the runway. It couldn't reach the speed it needed to get off the ground, ran out of runway, slithered through a fence and crashed into some buildings nearby.

Of the 44 people on board, 20 died at the scene. Three more succumbed to their injuries in the days that followed. In total, eight Manchester United players, three United staff members, two journalists and the aircraft's co-pilot perished. Two other United players were left with career-ending injuries.

The people who lost their lives on February 6, 1958 will never be forgotten by Manchester United. The way that the footballing community rallied around the team in the aftermath of the tragedy should also always be remembered.

Old Trafford has memorials to the tragedy including the Munich clock on the south east corner of the stadium which shows the time and date of the failed third take-off.

★ STEVE BRUCE ★

Steve Bruce started his professional career at Gillingham in 1979, moved to Norwich in 1984 and then Manchester United in 1987, helping strengthen the team at the back as well as knocking in more than his fair share of goals – mostly with his head.

He deputised frequently for captain Bryan Robson as the 1990s got underway and played a pivotal role in the United team that won three of the first four Premier League titles, as well as a European Cup Winner's Cup, three FA Cups, a League Cup, three Charity Shields (one of which was shared) and a European Super Cup.

Steve Bruce didn't play for England, but he did publish three murder mystery novels, *Striker!*, *Sweeper!* and Stadium Car Positioning Liaison Officer! (okay, it's actually *Defender!*), which apparently fetch an inexplicably pretty penny when they turn up at second-hand book sites. Possibly because he's buying them up to hide the evidence.

Moving swiftly on, Bruce went into management once his playing days were behind him, and has worked with several teams, including his boyhood club Newcastle United.

RESPECT THE BADGE: THE RED DEVIL ★ MANIFESTS ★

Manchester United can trace its history back for nearly a century and a half so, as you'd imagine, the club's badge has been through several changes over the years.

You won't be too surprised to discover that the early versions of the Newton Heath LYR FC team's badge featured a steam train and came in the corporate colours of the Lancashire and Yorkshire Railway. (You also probably won't be surprised to hear that in the 1880s the LYR's trains were able to make it over the Pennines more quickly than the current rail operators, but that's another tale for another time).

The badge became more recognisably 'football' in around 1891/92 when Newton Heath dropped the 'LYR' from its name and the steam train chugged off into the sunset; they were replaced with a shield with flourishes around it,

'LYR' was spelled out in a small font, the year of formation was added at the bottom and a football at the top. Watch that ball, it'll turn up again in 50 years.

When 1902 rolled around and Manchester United emerged from the chrysalis that was Newton Heath, the team simply took the crest of the city of Manchester as its badge, complete with Latin motto (concilio et labore: wisdom and effort), lions and unicorns rampant, red roses of the House of Lancaster and all sorts of other heraldic devices.

By the late 1940s, this was potentially becoming a little stuffy and staid (and difficult to sew on a shirt), so United simplified the badge, adopting something close to the modern version. Out went virtually everything from the council crest, with the exception of the three-masted sailing vessel, and in came a stylish, and presumably stylised, little red devil, brandishing a trident and staring deep into your soul. Thankfully, the devil was safely contained within a shield shaped like the one that adorned the old LYR crest. The football from the old Newton Heath logo bounced back, but rather than sitting atop the shield, there were now two of them, separating two stylised heraldic scroll type-things above and below the shield. These stylised heraldic scroll type-things contained the words 'Manchester United' above and 'Football Club' below. There were indecently large gaps between Manchester and United and Football and Club, but that aside, it certainly wasn't a million miles from the current badge. Everything came in a very spiffy red, black and white colour scheme. An instantly recognisable precursor of what we have today.

The sixties came along and the devil was exorcized, washed away by the three stripes that are said to represent the three rivers of Manchester and have graced the coats of arms of the Lords of Manchester since William the Conqueror's time.

In 1970, the colour scheme evolved from red and white into red and yellow and the topmost stylised heraldic scroll type-thing became somewhat rounder, and then, in 1973, the rivers drained away to reveal the devil once more.

And that's how things have stayed until today, with only a slight update in 1998 to ditch the words 'Football Club' from the bottom stylised heraldic scroll type-things so the top one just reads 'Manchester' and the bottom one just reads 'United', and to replace the white with a red background for the ship. Branding moves fast in this modern world.

"MAYBE ONE SMALL REGRET IS THAT I NEVER GOT TO PLAY WITH PAUL SCHOLES – BUT I WAS NEVER GOING TO LEAVE BARCELONA AND HE WAS NEVER GOING TO LEAVE MANCHESTER UNITED."

Xavi gazes to the north, mourning a love that that would never be.

★ ROY KEANE ★

It's the grit in the oyster that makes the pearl, and Roy Keane certainly brought the grit during his 12-and-a-half years at Old Trafford, giving the team an extra dynamic that basically screamed 'Do Not Mess' throughout the 1990s and early 2000s.

He amassed 326 Premier League and 480 overall appearances and won seven league titles. He also delivered 51 goals and numerous assists as he marshalled United from midfield.

He'd initially missed out on an apprenticeship in English football but was spotted by the mighty Brian Clough who took him to Nottingham Forest in 1990, where he spent three years before being enticed to his history-making role in the north-west.

Roy Keane once did two miraculous things in a match against Newcastle. Firstly, he made Alan Shearer's grin vanish by bouncing a ball off his head at a throw-in. Then he knocked the ensuing card out of the referee's hand while gesticulating(/taking a swing) at Shearer. This amazingly turned the card from yellow into red before our very eyes.

He left United for Celtic, where he spent six months before

retiring as a professional player. Alongside his exceptional role with United, Keane earned 67 caps for the Republic of Ireland, although he was, on occasion, quite scathing about the team set-up, which often made his relationships with the management quite challenging.

These days he works as an incisive – and occasionally tough to the point of scathing – pundit on television, amazing people with his ability to go from clean shaven at the start of a match to fully bearded by half-time.

TWO UNITED PLAYERS HAVE SCORED A DOUBLE HAT-TRICK IN A MATCH: HAROLD HALSE, AGAINST SWINDON TOWN IN SEPTEMBER 1911, AND GEORGE BEST AGAINST NORTHAMPTON TOWN IN FEBRUARY 1970.

"I'M NOT AT MANCHESTER UNITED TO KEEP EVERYONE HAPPY."

At a young age, Roy Keane showed the levels of incisive analysis that would latterly put him in such demand as a pundit.

THE OPPOSITION:
★ LEEDS ★

The rivalry between Manchester United and Leeds United is, in many ways, a bit weird. Yes, there was a time in the 1960s when both teams were challenging each other for various titles, both had respected managers and a Charlton brother. Then, in the 1970s, the tide went out on both teams and they were both struggling to maintain top division status, so their clashes took on a different complexion. Then, in the 1991/92 season, the pair were vying for supremacy in the First Division (Leeds won). But in the end, with the best will in the world, that's about it.

They didn't even play each other competitively until 1923, and that's not because there were a string of epic clashes with Leeds United's forebear, Leeds City (a long story involving financial irregularities meant that Leeds City ceased in 1919), as the pair only met twice in 1906 and avoided each other for the rest of their shared history. As of the end of the 2022/23 season, Leeds United and Manchester United have only played each other 113 times, with Manchester United winning nearly 45% of the time and drawing a third of the time.

Looking at the Premier League and Leeds haven't always featured, so the two teams have only played each other about half as often as Manchester United and Liverpool or Arsenal, for example. Either way, Manchester United have won nearly 70% of the matches at home and just under half of the matches at Elland Road.

Leeds fans also felt the loss of Eric Cantona very keenly, with the King's decision to move to Manchester seeming to confirm that there was a growing gap between the ambitions of the two clubs in the 1990s. His 90th minute goal against Leeds capped a 4-0 rout in 1996 and led to a sour journey home for the Yorkshire team's fans.

Despite there not being much in it on the pitch, the two sets of fans do have a history of setting each other off, singing unpleasant songs about tragedies that the others have suffered down the years. Unfortunately, both sides are as guilty as each other in this. It's just a bit sad for the families involved, really.

Not wanting to end things on a down point, it's worth noting that Sir Bobby Charlton has made Manchester United's most appearances against Leeds, while his brother Jack has made the joint most appearances for Leeds against Manchester United. It's a nice bit of symmetry if nothing else.

RUUD VAN NISTELROOIJ ONCE SCORED IN 10 CONSECUTIVE MATCHES, A UNITED RECORD.

"MY MIND WAS ALWAYS SET ON JOINING MANCHESTER UNITED. HOW CAN YOU NOT GO TO UNITED? I DON'T PLAY FOR MONEY. I PLAY FOR GLORY AND WINNING CHAMPIONSHIPS. I'M HAPPY HERE. I HEAR PEOPLE COMPLAIN ABOUT THE WEATHER, THERE'S NOTHING TO DO AND THE FOOD. BUT, FOR ME, IT'S NOT LIKE THAT. I PLAY FOR A CLUB I LOVE, THE BIGGEST CLUB, AND EVERYTHING ELSE DOESN'T MATTER."

Dimitar Berbatov, a man who never minded buying waterproofs, an Xbox and hiring chefs.

111

★ THE GAP ★

Sometimes you look at a measure and it's telling you something that you already know, but perhaps don't really want to hear.

The chart below shows the gap between the winning number of points in each season and the number that Manchester United accumulated in each season of the Premier League. United were so devastatingly successful for the two decades between 1992/93 and 2012/13 that the return to mortality over the last decade stands out like a sore thumb (which is a technical term often used in complex mathematical analysis).

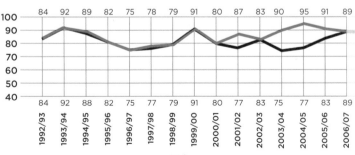

For 17 of the 21 seasons between 1992/93 and 2012/13, United were either top or within a point of being top. It's a phenomenal achievement.

The problem with being the best for such a long period, particularly when something like the creation of the Premier League offers a natural inflection point in history, is when that period moves into the history books, the cold reality hurts all the more. Especially when it's the noisy neighbours who have taken your place at the top of the pile.

What made the period from the early 1990s stand out was not just the manager, but also the youth players coming through; a selection of astute signings, the belief and – frankly – the right amount of competition to make the team strive to keep delivering. Some of those things you can control, some you can't ...

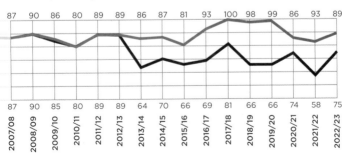

| | 87 | 90 | 86 | 80 | 89 | 89 | 86 | 87 | 81 | 93 | 100 | 98 | 99 | 86 | 93 | 89 |
| 87 | 90 | 85 | 80 | 89 | 89 | 64 | 70 | 66 | 69 | 81 | 66 | 66 | 74 | 58 | 75 |

2007/08 2008/09 2009/10 2010/11 2011/12 2012/13 2013/14 2014/15 2015/16 2016/17 2017/18 2018/19 2019/20 2020/21 2021/22 2022/23

★ PETER SCHMEICHEL ★

If you have an assertive team that has an instinct to attack (and attack and attack), you also need to be certain you've got a stable base both to build on and protect you – on the rare occasions that an attack breaks down. Peter Schmeichel offered that base for eight phenomenally successful years between 1991 and 1999.

There are those who think signing Eric Cantona was Alex Ferguson's best bit of business, but Ferguson himself points to the £505,000 signing of Schmeichel from Danish side Brøndby as his most astute move.

Most Vikings, of course, only came to these shores to trade, but there's a certain corner of the primal British brain that is instinctively terrified when challenged by a fast-moving 193 cm-tall bellowing blond bloke from the other side of the North Sea. It may be that Schmeichel tapped into that tribal memory, because he delivered 180 clean sheets in his 398 appearances, a record that has only just been surpassed more than two decades later by David de Gea.

Schmeichel also received 129 caps for Denmark, helping the country win the European Championships in 1992.

RED IN ALL KINDS
★ OF WAYS ★

Organised, association football, started out in the 1870s as a game for amateurs and gentlemen in some of the more refined parts of the south of England. It had somehow found its way to the north and ran rampant, turned professional and started doing something that few members of the aristocracy had intended or wanted: providing entertainment for the hoi polloi.

By the turn of the 20th century, football had transcended its less-than-humble roots, but the more regressive economic attitudes of the time were still rife in the game's regulatory authorities. Salary caps, rather than the free market, were used to keep wages in check, but they were so low that players didn't get a living wage. Contracts also didn't offer anything in the way of financial support if a player was injured during a match. There are several tales of players being injuries during a match and subsequently dying because they were unable to afford simple medical treatment. And families weren't supported after they were gone.

Players from Manchester United, supported by proudly self-made chairman John Henry Davies, decided to form a union to try to give football's leadership structure a group to negotiate with and reduce the growing tension within the sport about player treatment. It grew quickly, attracting significant support among the playing community across the country.

With the 1909/10 season on the horizon, talk of strikes among players started rumbling around and the footballing authorities decided to clamp down rather than discuss their grievances. Players were told to disband the union or face suspension. The threat initially worked, and many players were intimidated into leaving the union, but several United players stood firm, continuing to train, despite their enforced suspension.

A photo of them appeared in the newspapers training under the hastily scrawled banner of 'The Outcasts FC', which generated a lot of publicity and several players from other teams re-joined the union. The authorities were forced to back down and to start negotiating better contracts with the players.

It seems there's been a long tradition of taking a stand on the red side of Manchester.

★ DAVID BECKHAM ★

In the days before he became a global icon who seems to spend his time simply popping up in places in a variety of hairstyles, David Beckham was an impressive footballer.

He joined Manchester United in 1991, having come through the Tottenham Hotspur academy, and his first taste of major success came in 1992 when he won the FA Youth Cup playing alongside emerging talents Nicky Butt, Ryan Giggs, Gary and Phil Neville and Paul Scholes. Sporadic first team appearances and a brief but fruitful loan to Preston North End saw him cement a position in United's first team, and after that the titles basically kept coming.

He went on to make 265 league appearances for United, delivering 62 goals and something in the region of 44,000,561 assists (this might or might not be an exaggeration).

It's always fairly difficult to judge the reasons why a relationship starts to break down, but in the latter part of his United career, Beckham locked horns with Sir Alex Ferguson, with the manager suggesting that the player was too focused on his life outside of football as a celebrity and young father. The challenge is that to be the very best you need to train, train and train some more. At the same time, fathers also have a responsibility to play a role in their families. To be fair, though, there was never really any sign of a dip in Beckham's performances on the field or in his commitment to the club.

It's possible that Beckham's position as a modern role model and all-round metrosexual marked an inflection point between the macho, male-dominated world of the past and a more evenly balanced society where the roles of everyone in a relationship are similarly valued. It's also possible to read entirely too much into the tribulations of a successful footballer who had a gaffer who wouldn't accept anything less than total commitment.

Either way, Beckham left United in 2003, spent four successful years at Real Madrid before heading off to seek more fame and fortune in the US. He also had an excellent career with England, winning 115 caps and scoring 17 times, including that last-gasp free kick that took England through to the World Cup in 2002.

"ALL THEY CAN TALK ABOUT IS MANCHESTER UNITED,"

says Alex Ferguson, although one suspects that he didn't speak about much else either.

·MANCHESTER UNITED·

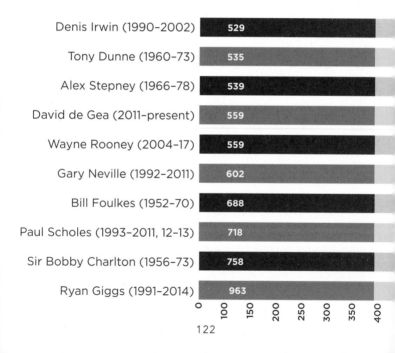

Player	Appearances
Denis Irwin (1990–2002)	529
Tony Dunne (1960–73)	535
Alex Stepney (1966–78)	539
David de Gea (2011–present)	559
Wayne Rooney (2004–17)	559
Gary Neville (1992–2011)	602
Bill Foulkes (1952–70)	688
Paul Scholes (1993–2011, 12–13)	718
Sir Bobby Charlton (1956–73)	758
Ryan Giggs (1991–2014)	963

0 100 150 200 250 300 350 400

122

MAN UTD'S TOP TEN FIRST TEAM ★ APPEARANCES ★

(ALL COMPETITIONS)

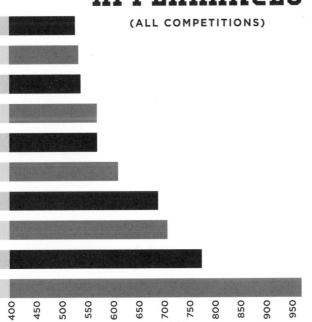

400 450 500 550 600 650 700 750 800 850 900 950 1000

★ GARY NEVILLE ★

The Neville family appear to be quite good at sport: Gary Neville's father played professional cricket, his sister is a netball international and his brother played alongside him at Manchester United for 11 years.

Neville captained the Manchester United youth team that won the FA Youth Cup in 1991/92 and made his senior debut in 1992. As a defender, he wasn't prolific in front of goal, but he does have five to his name – one of which was the 1,000th goal of Alex Ferguson's reign, which, if nothing else, is a fantastic pub quiz fact.

He made 400 league and 602 total appearances for Manchester United, and was the fifth club captain to lift the Premier League title, having taken the armband when Roy Keane moved himself on in November 2005/06.

He was also one of the first names on the England team sheet, earning 85 caps between 1995 and 2007.

He retired from professional football in 2011, having spent his entire playing career with United. He is now a regular face on television, and on a good day appears to relish being more outspoken than Graeme Souness.

ACCEPT NO
★ SUBSTITUTES ★

The rules of football have developed over time, and sometimes it's a surprise when you realise that the things we take for granted today weren't introduced until relatively late in the game's development.

Case in point: substitutes. Substitutes were allowed in the earliest days of the game in the event that a player failed to turn up for a match, but it wasn't actually until 1958 that replacement players, in the way that we understand them today, were allowed – and it's possible that Manchester United played a role in their introduction.

In 1957, United won the league and were only denied a double by Aston Villa in the FA Cup. The Busby Babes fielded the youngest team ever for a Cup final, but they were favourites to win. In the sixth minute of the match, though, United goalie Ray Wood was stretchered off with a broken cheekbone after a clash with the Villa outside left. These days, the clash in question would probably have led to a yellow card at the very least for the Villa player, given that Wood had the ball under control in his hands when he was charged into. Either way, it was United that had to limp on with 10 men until a visibly dazed Wood was reintroduced, because this was in the days before substitutes (let alone modern niceties like concussion checks).

The year before and it was Manchester City in the FA Cup final, and without going into too much detail, their goalie, Bert Trautmann, also suffered from a collision with an opposition player. He too played through the pain so as not to let his team down, although it was later discovered that he'd broken his neck in the collision.

1958 saw FIFA change the rules of the game and substitutes were formally allowed in the event of an injury to a goalkeeper and one other outfield player. It took a few more years before the FA adopted the changes, with substitutions becoming part of the game in the 1965/66 season.

This might all feel like a long time ago, when the world was all in black and white and everybody spoke terribly, terribly poshly, but it's worth remembering that it was eight decades after the game first formalised its rules, which is a long time to go without substitutes, particularly given the way that tackles used to fly.

The rules were updated to allow two substitutes in 1988, and three in 1995, with further allowances made during the Covid-19 pandemic. There is a perfect point between having the right number of substitutes to allow a manager to respond to injuries and letting teams waste time at the end of a match by making several substitutions. It is possible that the perfect point will never be found.

NEWTON HEATH'S FIRST COMPETITIVE MATCH WAS A 2-7 DEFEAT TO BLACKBURN OLYMPIC RESERVES IN THE LANCASHIRE CUP IN OCTOBER 1883. COMPETITIVE IS RELATIVE.

"I SPENT A LOT OF MONEY ON BOOZE, BIRDS AND FAST CARS. THE REST I JUST SQUANDERED."

It wasn't a cliché until George Best said it.

★ TEDDY SHERINGHAM ★

130

How, actually, do you follow Eric Cantona? Who on earth could replace the flamboyant Frenchman, not only in terms of footballing capabilities but also in the hearts and minds of the Manchester United faithful?

The short answer is that you can't, but Teddy Sheringham came along after Cantona retired, joining from Tottenham Hotspur and bringing a completely different, but no lesser, quality to United. After a slightly quiet start, he found his feet (and the back of the net) and went on to help United win the title in 1998/99, and then came off the bench to score the opening goal in the victorious FA Cup final. He capped off the treble-winning season by scoring the equaliser and then delivering the assist for Ole Gunnar Solskjær's winner in a dramatic European Champions League final. Consecutive league titles followed in 1999/2000 and 2000/01.

With the arrival of Ruud van Nistelrooij and with his four-year contract at an end, he called time on his Old Trafford days and went back from whence he came, legendary status achieved, trophies to prove it.

THE OPPOSITION:
★ ARSENAL ★

For a second it looked like it might be Blackburn, and then for a brief moment it looked like it could be Newcastle, but in the end, it was the north Londoners who rose to put in a consistent challenge to United's hegemony of the Premier League in the 1990s. Even now, nearly two decades after the rivalry was at its height, United vs Arsenal tends to be one of the jewels in any football season's crown.

The two teams have faced each other 238 times since Newton Heath faced off against Woolwich Arsenal in a 3–3 nail-biter back in 1894. United have had the better of it, winning over 40% of the time and drawing slightly more than 20% of the time. The other thing happened just under 40% of the time.

Looking at the Premier League era, United have won over 40% of the matches that they have played against Arsenal, but splitting it out by home and away, and the Old Trafford advantage is clear: United win just under 60% of matches at home. The downside of this is that they have only won around a quarter of the time at either of the Arsenal stadiums. Equally, if you are lucky enough to have a ticket to see the two teams meet in the Premier League, you have a 25% chance of seeing four or more goals.

This may be a contentious statement, but it's worth remembering that no matter how tense a football match becomes, who says what and who tries to do what to whom, it is just a game. Roy Keane and Arsenal's Patrick Viera were the focal point of many of the angriest stand-offs between United and the Gunners in the mid-1990s to early 2000s, but the pair have managed to grow past their differences and were recently spotted out having an ice cream together. Onlookers said that they could see flowers come into bloom as the pair walked past, birds started singing a little louder, and at one point there was even a beautiful rainbow in the background ... And then they went and spoiled it all by having a tiff over who paid.

WEIRDLY, THE RECORD CROWD FOR A MATCH AT OLD TRAFFORD WASN'T SET BY A MANCHESTER UNITED GAME. IN 1939, 76,962 SPECTATORS WATCHED THE FA CUP SEMI-FINAL BETWEEN WOLVERHAMPTON WANDERERS AND GRIMSBY TOWN.

"FERGIE SAID I WAS A MANCHESTER UNITED PLAYER IN THE WRONG SHIRT—I SAID HE WAS AN ARSENAL MANAGER IN THE WRONG BLAZER."

If current theories about the multiverse are correct, there are realities where Tony Adams played for Manchester United and Sir Alex Ferguson managed the Gunners. It's something to think about ...

★ RIO FERDINAND ★

Scouted by Frank Lampard Sr, Rio Ferdinand joined the West Ham youth set-up in 1992, graduating to the first team three years later. He then spent a couple of seasons in Leeds from November 2000 before joining Manchester United at the start of the 2002/03 season.

He stayed at Old Trafford for 12 years, making 455 appearances and delivering a smattering of goals. He was also capped 81 times for England, representing the country at several international tournaments.

Ferdinand would never have made it as a professional dancer because apparently his hamstrings are not long enough, but what he gained from four years of ballet training reinforced his natural balance, poise, strength and resilience. He also represented the London Borough of Southwark in gymnastics at the London Youth Games when he was 11. Given that he hails from Peckham in south-east London, you'd assume he learned early on to deal with the people who thought they'd try to take the mickey.

He holds the honour of scoring Manchester United's last goal at Old Trafford under Alex Ferguson. Since retiring, he has gone on to become an insightful football pundit and has used his national profile to campaign on a range of issues.

THE OPPOSITION:
★ CHELSEA ★

Life can be a funny old thing; you are going along perfectly happily expecting another year of tense stand-offs with Arsenal, when all of a sudden, out of the blue, it's west London's most aspirational who suddenly decide they are going to start trying to clamber over everyone else and take the title.

Chelsea and Manchester United have been playing each other on and off since 1905, a 0–0 draw on Christmas day.

They have faced each other 192 times, with United winning a little over 40% of the time, but up until the turn of the century they'd rubbed along relatively amicably: two teams that had had their share of trials and tribulations but had never really both been in the ascendancy at the same time.

That changed at the start of the new millennium, with Chelsea suddenly challenging for a seat at the top table. They pulled together a string of good teams and had a manager who thought he had the lyrical flair to try to play mind games in the media with Alex Ferguson. It made life interesting, if nothing else.

The manager in question did take up residence in Old Trafford briefly. He ruffled a few feathers, as is his way, and then moved on fairly quickly. He was thanked for his input and, of course, wished well.

Since the creation of the Premier League, the two sides have drawn a little over 40% of the time, Chelsea have won around 30% of the time and United just under that. Breaking it down to pre- and post-2003/04 season when Chelsea's fortunes (and fortune) dramatically improved, pre-2003/04, games between the two teams ended evens just under half the time, Chelsea won around a quarter of the time and United around 30% of the time. Since 2003/04, draws have become less frequent, only occurring around 40% of the time, with Chelsea winning around a third of the time and United winning around a quarter of the time.

Generally, Manchester United vs Chelsea is a low-scoring affair, with fewer than two and a half goals scored on average when the pair meet in the Premier League, and the game deflating to a nervy 0–0 draw more than 10% of the time. In the more than 60 matches that the two teams have played in the Premier League, you only get more than five or more goals around 10% of the time.

The reason United vs Chelsea matches tend to be nervy affairs is because no matter what state the teams are in, at any point after December, one or the other of them will be in with a shout of chasing down the title. They tend to want to stand in each other's way rather than try to blow each other away.

"A REGRET? THAT I NEVER PLAYED FOR MANCHESTER UNITED, I'D HAVE LIKED THAT."

Czech legend and Juventus stalwart Pavel Nedvěd speaks for all of us. We'd all have liked to see him play for United and we'd all like to play for United.

★ CRISTIANO RONALDO ★

Ronaldo joined Manchester United in 2003 and very quickly established himself as a goal-scoring phenomenon, becoming the leading Premier League goal scorer in three consecutive years. This includes 2007/08 when he walloped 31 league goals into the back of the net, a season tally that eclipses every other United player since the formation of the Premier League.

Ronaldo left Manchester for Spain in 2009, enjoying the best part of a decade with Real Madrid before moving on to Italy's Juventus. He was welcomed back to Manchester United in 2021. He was once again United's top Premier League goal scorer, but at the back end of 2022 he made the decision to speak out about how he felt the club was being run and left by mutual consent shortly afterwards.

He has been without doubt one of the greatest footballers of his generation, and he would have a strong case to make for being in an all-time world 11: in the years that he was playing at Old Trafford, there were an awful lot of Monday morning conversations that included the phrase, "Yeah, but did you see what Ronaldo did?"

MANCHESTER UNITED
★ WFC ★

The history of men's football is long and convoluted, so in some ways it's quite refreshing that the history of women's football is relatively short – as a result of the FA's decision to ban women's teams from using official facilities between 1920 and the early 1970s. It's still convoluted, though.

Case in point, Manchester United WFC …

Back in the 1970s, Manchester United Supporters Club Ladies started up, they grew a bit and became founding members of one of the regional leagues that were set up in the late 1980s. The team kept growing and, by 2001, formed an official partnership with Manchester United proper. In 2005, shortly after a change in corporate leadership at United overall, the plug was pulled on the women's team because it wasn't part of the club's core business.

Fast forward to 2018 and United were one of the few teams in the Premier League that didn't have a women's organisation, so they did the decent thing and set up Manchester United WFC, bringing in former Lioness Casey Stoney as head coach.

Presumably reflecting the fact that United had some serious making up to do, Stoney brought with her a significant amount of credibility, having been capped 130 times for England and played at Arsenal (two stints), Charlton Athletic, Chelsea, Lincoln and Liverpool during a two-decade professional career.

Stoney guided United to two consecutive fourth positions in the Women's Super League before resigning. Marc Skinner has replaced her and has delivered an impressive second place in the 2022/23 season, so it looks like the team's going from strength to strength.

It may be that the Lionesses' success at Euro 2022 – and the fact that the Manchester derby attracted more than 30,000 fans within the first 12 months of Manchester United WFC being set up – will encourage corporate management teams to keep supporting the women's game; there is clearly both an appetite and an opportunity for women's football.

★ ERIC CANTONA ★

A football team is a group of players all doing different things in pursuit of a single objective or goal. Within that, some players have a little more personality than others; some, you might even go so far as to say, have character. Someone who definitely has a surfeit of character is Eric Cantona.

It's one thing to be a legend in your own head, but it's a feat of personality to become Eric Cantona – the man so cool he played with his collars up and we all just shrugged and let him get on with it. He could have lined up in a red and yellow top hat and we'd all just have said, "Yeah, he looks good." If any of the rest of us mortals started to saunter around with our collars up like he did, two things would happen.

1. We'd be ridiculed.

2. We'd be forgotten.

Not Cantona. For five years, he strode around Old Trafford, collars aloft, Fergie's general, delivering 64 goals in 143 league appearances.

His £1 million fee to join United from Leeds was relatively humble, even by the standards of the day (although it was allegedly reported to be higher to keep Leeds fans happy). It might qualify as the best bit of business Ferguson ever did, because his arrival galvanised the team, instilling a level of confidence in the younger players that gave them the space to develop.

There were, it's fair to say, moments where his braggadocio went over the top, and he was often targeted by opposition players – and sometimes fans – as they tried to get a rise out of him. When cooler heads took over, though, his responses were considered, sanguine and mature and, on one occasion, famously philosophical (it involved seagulls, trawlers and a range of bemused journalists trying to make sense of their notes).

Since retirement he's worked steadily as an actor, but he has also turned out as player-coach of the French national beach football team – they took both the 2004 Euro Beach Soccer League title and the FIFA Beach Soccer World Cup in 2005. Why not?

"I AM VERY HAPPY AND VERY PROUD AND AT THE SAME TIME, I AM NOT SURPRISED,"

said Eric Cantona on being told he had been inducted into the Premier League Hall of Fame.

THE OPPOSITION:
★ MANCHESTER CITY ★

So then, the noisy neighbours. The other half of the
Manchester derby, a match that's been played since 1881.
The Etihad is in the Manchester suburb of Bradford which
has undergone significant regeneration over the last few
years

The easiest way to tell the story of the rivalry between
United and City is probably to stick to the facts. And the

facts are that United has won a little over 40% of the meetings between the two, and City have won a little over 30%.

There has also been a significant change in fortunes for both teams over the last decade and a half, first as a result of the new ownership at City, which took over in 2008, and then United going through a period of uncertainty following the retirement of Alex Ferguson in 2013.

Interestingly, when you drill down into the data, while the balance of power has clearly changed, it's not as strongly in favour of City as you might expect. Prior to 2008, United won more than half of the matches that the two teams played in the Premier League, while City won around a quarter. After the takeover of City, they now win a little over 40% of the matches, and United win the same percentage. Just under 15% of matches end in a draw.

You've also got a decent chance of seeing goals, with an average of nearly three per match through the history of the Premier League, and a nearly 30% chance of seeing four or more goals when the two sides of Manchester come together. You've also got a 10% chance of a 0-0 though, so take a book, just in case.

The bottom line, though, is that if you are looking for entertainment, for high-stakes football played with a bit of swagger, you could do much worse than head to Manchester on derby day. If you can get hold of tickets.

WAYNE ROONEY HOLDS THE RECORD FOR THE MOST GOALS SCORED BY AN ENGLISH PLAYER IN THE CHAMPION'S LEAGUE WITH 30 GOALS. PAUL SCHOLES IS THIRD WITH 24. ROONEY IS JOINT 26TH AND SCHOLES JOINT 45TH IN THE OVERALL TABLE. CRISTIANO RONALDO IS THE HIGHEST SCORER WITH 140, FOLLOWED BY LIONEL MESSI WITH 129.

**"I JUST WANT TO GET
IN THE TEAM AND
SHOW ALL OF THEM
WHAT I CAN DO,"**

explained Wayne Rooney when
he signed for Manchester United.
Fair to say that it worked out.

★ WAYNE ROONEY ★

Wayne Rooney started his playing career with Everton, the club he supported as a child, where he made possibly the most important contribution to English football that a player could ever make – coming off the bench to score the goal that ended Arsenal's 30-match unbeaten run in October 2002. It was a goal that meant Liverpool went to the top of the league at Arsenal's expense, but this was the 2002/03 season so it all turned out fine in the end.

He joined Manchester United in the 2004/05 season, delivering a Champions League hat-trick on debut. He was still only 18 and appeared to have what might be called a promising future …

Over the 13 years he was with United, he became the club's record goal scorer, delivering 253 goals and an infinite number of assists. He is also the Premier League's third highest scorer for a single club after Harry Kane and Sergio Agüero.

He also worked tirelessly for England, making 120 appearances, finding the net 53 times to become England's top international scorer until he was surpassed by Harry Kane at the start of 2023.

With his playing days behind him, he has taken his skills into management.

Player	Club		Caps
Bryan Robson	West Bromwich Albion, Manchester United, Middlesborough		
Billy Wright	Wolverhampton Wanderers		
Frank Lampard	West Ham, Chelsea, Manchester City		
Bobby Charlton	Manchester United		
Ashley Cole	Arsenal, Chelsea, Derby County		
Bobby Moore	West Ham, Fulham		
Steven Gerrard	Liverpool		
David Beckham	Manchester United		
Wayne Rooney	Everton, Manchester United, Derby County		
Peter Shilton	Leicester City, Stoke City, Nottingham Forest, Southampton, Derby County, Plymouth Argyle, Wimbledon, Bolton Wanderers, Coventry City, West Ham United, Leyton Orient		

ENGLAND CAPS
CHART
★ CHART ★

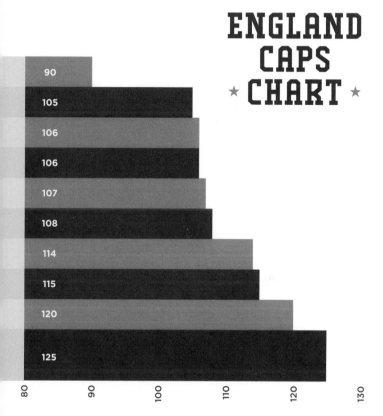

90	
105	
106	
106	
107	
108	
114	
115	
120	
125	

80 · 90 · 100 · 110 · 120 · 130

★ MARCUS RASHFORD ★

Marcus Rashford joined Manchester United at the tender age of seven, breaking through to the first team in the 2015/16 season. Smashing through might be more appropriate: he scored twice in his first team debut in the Europa League against Danish club Midtjylland, which is all well and good, but three days later he scored twice again in his Premier League debut. Against Arsenal.

He has also shone on the international stage as England's long-term plan to challenge for trophies has started to get tantalisingly close to fruition. He's already played for England 51 times, was included in the squad for the 2016 Euros, scored three minutes into his debut in a friendly against Australia, and has been one of the first names on the team sheet since Gareth Southgate took over as England manager.

Rashford has emerged as a leader, both on and off the field, giving United fans something to cheer when he's on the field and the rest of society something to think about when he's not. Who knows where his career will take him next, but there's no doubt that he's been a bright spot in a difficult few seasons for the club.

★ THE TROPHY CABINET ★

Competition	Year
First Division Premier League	1907/08, 1910/11, 1951/52, 1955/56, 1956/57, 1964/65, 1966/67, 1992/93, 1993/94, 1995/96, 1996/97, 1998/99, 1999/2000, 2000/01, 2002/03, 2006/07, 2007/08, 2008/09, 2010/11, 2012/13
Second Division	1935/36, 1974/75
FA Cup	1908/09, 1947/48, 1962/63, 1976/77, 1982/83, 1984/85, 1989/90, 1993/94, 1995/96, 1998/99, 2003/04, 2015/16
Football League Cup EFL Cup	1991/92, 2005/06, 2008/09, 2009/10, 2016/17, 2022/23
FA Charity Shield FA Community Shield	1908, 1911, 1952, 1956, 1957, 1965*, 1967*, 1977*, 1983, 1990*, 1993, 1994, 1996, 1997, 2003, 2007, 2008, 2010, 2011, 2013, 2016 (*shared)
European Cup UEFA Champions League	1967/68, 1998/99, 2007/08
UEFA Europa League	2016/17
UEFA Super Cup	1991
European Cup Winners' Cup	1990/91
FIFA Club World Cup	2008
Intercontinental Cup	1999